Ian Heath's

HEArtS

For
Charlotte and Ben

summersdale

HEARTS

This edition published in 2010 by Summersdale Publishers Ltd.

First published by W. H. Allen & Co plc in 1984.

Copyright © Ian Heath, 1984.

Summersdale Publishers Ltd
46 West Street
Chichester
West Sussex
PO19 1RP
UK

www.summersdale.com

Printed and bound in China

ISBN: 978-1-84953-037-8

Substantial discounts on bulk quantities of Summersdale books are available to corporations, professional associations and other organisations. For details telephone Summersdale Publishers on (+44-1243-771107), fax (+44-1243-786300) or email (nicky@summersdale.com).

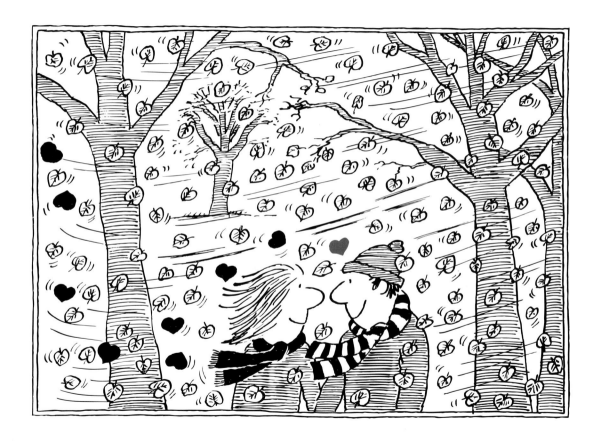

. . . .

. . . .

Have you enjoyed this book? If so, why not write a review on your favourite website?

Thanks very much for buying this Summersdale book.

www.summersdale.com